Herman Wells
Stories

Herman B Wells with three symbols of his Indiana University
presidency—school bell, globe of the world, and begging bowl.

Herman Wells
Stories

❖

A S
T O L D   B Y
H I S   F R I E N D S
O N   H I S   90th   B I R T H D A Y

Edited by

John Gallman, Rosann Greene,
Jim Weigand, and Doug Wilson

Indiana University Press

BLOOMINGTON *&* INDIANAPOLIS

CONTENTS

Preface

This book cannot be characterized as even an informal biography of the man named Herman B (no period) Wells. Rather, through the personal recollections of people whose lives he has touched, it seeks to capture in some small way the essence of the man who, far more than anyone else, built Indiana University into the distinguished institution of higher learning that it is today.

It was a most enjoyable project. Reading through the anecdotes is a warm and nostalgic amble through the past. Each tale, in its own way, recalls a special time or place in the history of the University while at the same time illustrates Chancellor Wells' distinctive and usually unique response to whatever the issue, event, or person at hand.

Given the immense number of people who have come into contact with Chancellor Wells during his long, long association with the University, the task of collecting, reading, editing, and organizing the contents of this book was initially daunting. Only through the efforts and able assistance of many people could the project have been completed. To all of them go the heartfelt thanks of the editors of the publication. And our appreciation for those who took the time to prepare the personal narratives included in this volume is enormous!

Each story, or in some cases a group of several stories, is followed by the name of the contributor. The stories are arranged by alphabetical order of the contributors' names. On the occasion of their reunion in June 1991, the former houseboys who over the years had worked for Chancellor Wells had a similar idea and prepared the booklet "Herman Wells Reminiscences"; some of those special recollections are included also in this 90th-birthday celebration.

We know, of course, that there are many untold stories. If after reading these pages you would like to share a special experience about Chancellor Wells, we encourage you to submit it to the office of the Vice President of University Relations. Thought is being given to preparing a second edition and new contributions would be most welcome.

Finally, we urge you to remember that this is a collection of stories. The volume does not attempt to portray the definitive Wells. He has touched too many lives in too many ways for that to be possible. Anyone who has come into contact with the man knows his or her own Wells and we know that each is equally authentic.

JIM WEIGAND

Herman Wells
Stories

"There Might Even Be Fisticuffs!"

THE occasion was the alumni barbecue. The scene was the beloved tree-shaded Well House in the center of the Bloomington campus. In his speech, Dr. Wells was lavish in praise for his successor, Dr. Elvis Stahr. After the genuine warmth of his welcome to this Indiana University newcomer, he pounded his fist on the table. The crowd went noticeably silent. "And Mr. President, if I ever hear of any tree cutting going on, I will most assuredly take off this friendly hat of approval and as an outraged alumnus go after you—there might even be fisticuffs!" The laughter of the crowd rang out almost as loudly as the carillon in the clock tower.

Memorial Stadium

THE project being planned was the Memorial Stadium, a new facility for football games. The mood was broadly and strongly in opposition to a new stadium, but the project was strongly supported by Dr. Wells. The prevailing spirit was that since we could not fill the stadium we had, why build a new one? As time has passed, once again the forward thinking of our leader has demonstrated his wisdom. The then existing stadium has long since crumbled and disappeared into a memorial arboretum; the current stadium has become the site for exciting athletics and, in recent years, memorable commencements. But on the opening day of the new Memorial Stadium as Indiana University and Michigan State University played the first game, Dr. Wells stood up in his seat very near to mine. He looked from corner to corner on both sides and turned to me and said, "Bill, I wonder what they are thinking now."

Football

FOOTBALL was not going well. On numerous occasions, Dr. Wells would enumerate the outstanding achievements of his beloved University. "I have tried to be a good president. How is it that we can have such a great school of music, outstanding schools of business, medicine, and dentistry, but we cannot win at football? I wish someone would tell me how."

"A House for Young People"

WHILE I served as President of the I.U. Foundation, I received many telephone calls from Dr. Wells asking if we could do this or that project, solve this or that problem. The biggest thrill in my memory was a call that came one week before Founders Day, the annual event that recognized students for academic achievement. Dr. Wells told the story of a 4.00 GPA student who could not attend the ceremony because he had no clothes. He did not want the student to miss Founders Day, could we help. We found it to be true, the young man had no suit, no tie. I have long remembered the thrill I got from seeing that young man walk across the stage in the Auditorium to receive his special greeting from Dr. Wells. And I have often recalled Dr. Wells' words: "We're not running a factory, we're running a house for young people, for good people."

Not for Sale

IN all my years of working with Dr. Wells, he rarely told me no. Instead, if he did not approve of or support my request, he just did not answer. I remember one occasion, however, early in my career, when he left no doubt about the decision. A doctor had come to me asking if the University could use a $1 million gift. A patient of his would consider it the greatest thing that could happen if he were to receive an honorary degree. Well, WSA went to HBW with the exciting news. The very second I finished my story, he jumped out of his chair, pounded his fist on the desk and said in no uncertain terms, "We do not sell honorary degrees, regardless of the amount. Go back and report this!"

Love of Life

I think of my friend and colleague, Dr. Wells, as a lover of people, a lover of life who never missed a wedding, a funeral, or a candy dish.

 WILLIAM S. ARMSTRONG

Finger Bowls

ONE dinner party was a bit unusual. After a course that required the use of one's fingers, finger bowls were given to each guest. One gentleman was apparently unfamiliar with their purpose and proceeded to pick up his spoon. At that moment Dr. Wells, with great alacrity and awareness, put his fingers in his bowl with flair and sound, thus saving the guest from the embarrassment of consuming his finger-bowl water.

 RONALD BALLENGER

On Memory

AT a meeting of the Distinguished Alumni Service Award (DASA) Club membership, Dr. Wells was reporting to us on the preparation of his book, *Being Lucky*. In the course of his report he came up with this comment, which I consider classic: "When you set out to do something like this book, it is amazing how many things you remember that never really happened."

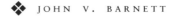

JOHN V. BARNETT

Mr. Eli

IN the early 1970s Eli Lilly called Herman Wells on the telephone. Mr. Eli told Herman that he was interested in making a gift to Indiana University and would like Herman to come to Indianapolis at his convenience to discuss the gift. As the story goes, Herman said, "I'll be there tomorrow."

Herman made arrangements to have an early supper with Mr. Eli at his Indianapolis home. When they met, Mr. Eli explained that he wished to give to Indiana University the four houses located on Sunset Lane in Indianapolis. It was Mr. Eli's intention that these houses be maintained in the same condition and used in the same manner as they had been used by the Lilly family over the years. He thought that Indiana University was the one institution which could see to this continuing interest of the Lilly family.

Mr. Eli also said that he knew how expensive it was to manage and maintain these four properties. He said it would be wrong if educational funds had to be diverted for the purpose of maintaining these homes. While Mr. Eli knew that the houses would be used for University functions, and as a residence for University officers, he said the University should create an endowment to pay all of these maintenance costs. To address that issue Mr. Eli said that he was going to make a cash gift the yield from which would pay the maintenance costs. He pulled out his small blue checkbook and wrote a check just as any of us would write a check for groceries. Mr. Eli put the check in an envelope and handed it to Herman. Herman, being the gentleman that he was, did not open the envelope to see the amount of the check. He simply put it in his coat pocket.

After the supper was over, Herman left Mr. Eli's house and, as he tells it, stopped under what was the first street light to open the envelope. He discovered that it was a check for $1 million, drawn on a simple bank check form. And this was in 1972, when a million dollars was still a lot of money.

 JERRY BEPKO

Even in Thailand

PERHAPS my favorite personal anecdote about Dr. Wells that astounded me at the time and that conveys one element of his impact—the worldwide recognition he has brought to Indiana University—occurred when the late George Pinnell and I were in Bangkok in 1970 (he as Dean of the School of Business and me as his Associate Dean). The Thai National Institute of Development Administration held a reception and luncheon in our honor. During the reception we were brought over to a tall, distinguished gentleman who was introduced to us as Prince Wan Waithayakon. He was the uncle of the King of Thailand. His first words to us were: "How is Herman?" We responded that he was quite well, thank you. Then he said, "And how is his mother?"

 CHARLES F. BONSER

Hermie

I do not recall the exact date or the exact building on the I.U. campus in which this occurred. To me it represents the respect and admiration that students and adult visitors held for Herman Wells. He was President of the University at the time. Dr. Wells was walking through one of the classroom buildings and was met about the same time by an adult visitor and a student. The visitor greeted Dr. Wells by saying "Good Morning, President Wells" and the student said "Hi, Hermie." Dr. Wells returned each of their greetings with a big smile and a "Good Morning."

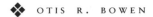 OTIS R. BOWEN

Pocket Money

ONE day in the early sixties I accompanied Herman to New York on a grant-seeking trip for support of an honors pre-med program. As the taxi from the airport drew up in front of the St. Regis Hotel, Herman said to me, "Oh my goodness, I forgot to bring any money." I offered the modest contents of my billfold, only to be told not to worry. As the doorman opened the taxi door, he said, "Welcome to the St. Regis, President Wells." Herman's reply: "Thank you, Charles. Will you please go in and ask the cashier for money to pay the cab driver?" It was done. Herman didn't need pocket money to travel.

Honey and Spice

ONE day in the late fifties, Sam Will, then Chairman of the French Department, came to my office in Arts and Sciences to complain about some act of the administration. I said, "Sam, I really think you should go to President Wells about this." Sam's reply: "I wouldn't dare. He'd charm me!"

Braden's Revenge

A midlevel I.U. administrator received an inquiry from the president of an eastern state university about the I.U. person's availability to be considered for a deanship. One thing led to another, and the administrator received a flattering offer to leave. Before accepting, however, the administrator asked for an interview to tell President Wells about the offer. "Do you know who recommended you for the post?" President Wells asked. "No, and I wondered," said the I.U. candidate. "Well, I did," said Wells, "and you are not to accept it!" So I didn't.

 SAMUEL E. BRADEN

Not Just Lucky

As a leader, Herman Wells has many skills. Outstanding among these, in my opinion, are his ability to work toward consensus before there is public confrontation and his keen sense of timing.

Of course, there were differences of opinion about some of his proposals. But the hours spent phoning and meeting with key figures involved in a potential controversy prior to an action by the faculty, the Trustees, or the General Assembly—touching all bases, considering arguments of opponents, giving background information to proponents—in all lessening the grounds for public argument, which tends to get people boxed into positions.

The art of timing has been demonstrated in many ways, but one example is publication of the Kinsey reports. It was more than coincidence that those books came out after the legislative session ended, not during or just before. By the time of the next session any public furor—and there was always some—had died down and a possible issue had been defused.

❖ ROBERT E. BURTON

The 25th Rose

ONE of my favorite stories concerns the 25 roses President Wells sent to Branch McCracken on his retirement after 24 years as basketball coach. Mrs. McCracken happened to count them. When she told Herman he had 25 roses rather than 24, he replied that he had included his year of service in the Navy during World War II, which he considered service to the University as well.

"Next Question!"

ANOTHER memory involves President Wells' chairing a large meeting in the Auditorium on a very contentious issue, which I have forgotten. When someone in the audience raised a disgraceful question, Herman passed right by and responded, "Next question!"

Of Names and Children

WHEN Sister Madelena, President of St. Mary's College, died and Herman prepared to fly to South Bend for the funeral, he invited me and our daughter Sally, then a student at St. Mary's, to go with him. He knew that I knew Sister Madelena well, but I cannot imagine how he learned, or remembered, that Sally was a student there. This is typical of his thoughtfulness and incredible memory. He even remembered the names and identities of each of our seven children.

Borrowed Expression

WHEN I came to Bloomington late in the winter of 1956 for an interview in the History Department, the chairman arranged for me to meet Mr. Wells in his office for ten minutes. The session lasted a very pleasant and intellectually stimulating forty minutes. I was trying to measure the University's commitment to increasing research and instruction on Russia and Eastern Europe and the rest of the so-called non-Western world. The knowledge I had of his career and interests from men I knew in the Ford and Rockefeller Foundations had given me some assurance. But when he described the University's programs, especially overseas, he convinced me. Finally, he remarked that the campus of the University was not just in Bloomington or even the state of Indiana, but included the world. Then, typically, he remarked that he had borrowed the expression from the president of the University of Wisconsin who had defined the world as the university's campus.

❖   ROBERT F. BYRNES

9

"Jimtown"

I had heard stories about Dr. Wells' love of driving, but when I worked for him as a houseboy in the late 1970s he relied mainly on the services of a full-time chauffeur. Sometimes he drove himself to campus and to church, and occasionally on longer trips. On one hot summer Sunday he invited me to accompany him to Jamestown, his birthplace in Boone County, where many of his relatives still lived. He suggested that he pilot the big blue Oldsmobile 98 on the 90-mile trip north and I handle the return journey. Somewhere past Martinsville we veered off the main highway as Dr. Wells decided to take the scenic route. As we traveled through the bucolic Hoosier countryside with the windows wide open, Dr. Wells kept up a steady stream of commentary and a speed of 75 miles an hour. More concerned with safety than with scenery, I could hardly take my eyes from the road, and I mentally prepared myself for the worst. Here I was hurtling along with the septuagenarian Chancellor of Indiana University, who could barely see over the steering wheel and seemed to be paying more attention to his travelogue than to the lane markers. After a while I decided it was useless to worry and adopted a fatalistic attitude. If this was to be my last day, why not enjoy the sun, the wind, and the exhilarating fellowship? We arrived at Jamestown—or "Jimtown," as Dr. Wells liked to call it—without incident, and spent a pleasant afternoon visiting his relatives. As I drove Dr. Wells back to Bloomington that evening, I reflected on my good fortune to have glimpsed his legendary spirit set free yet another time by the open road.

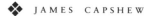 JAMES CAPSHEW

Roll, Jordan, Roll

DURING the 1950s while serving as Academic Dean of the then I.U. Extension Center, during a summer vacation period I had a conference with President Herman B Wells. Many of the faculty, staff, and students were off campus, including some members of his staff. President Wells was late. On arrival, however, he gave ample reason for having been tardy. An addition to the Indiana Memorial Union was in progress, and the President reported that he had been on a mission to save the Jordan River. Some, he explained, wanted to cover a portion of the Jordan River. Then, with emphasis, indicating resolve and determination, the President said, "The Jordan River is going to remain on campus so long as I am here!" And so it has, and so it will doubtless continue to trickle by the Indiana Memorial Union.

Every generation of students from the 1930s onward has had much evidence to indicate that keeping the campus attractive and beautiful has always been a very high priority with Herman B Wells. After he became Chancellor it was Herman B Wells who led and pressed the effort which resulted in the heart of the older part of the campus being placed on the State as well as the National Register of Historic Places.

❖ DONALD F. CARMONY

Fraternity Brother

A group of historians came to Bloomington for a business meeting. When we were finished with the meeting several of them said they had never seen the Indiana campus. This was in the 1969–70 era. I was driving them through campus when suddenly a whole

army of students marched across the road. Immediately the guests were certain they were witnessing a student rebellion. At the tail-end of the procession was Dr. Wells plowing along, not exactly in lock step. I assured my visitors that it was simply a parade of Sigma Nu brothers.

❖ THOMAS D. CLARK

The Secret Weapon

EARLY in my work with Dr. Wells, I learned that he does not indulge in introspection. He wastes little time reflecting on an event or a decision, asking himself how it could have been improved. Instead, as soon as an obligation is met, an engagement attended, a speech given, he begins thinking about the next items on his calendar. This trait has its virtues but it defies the interviewer trying to discover how Dr. Wells accomplished so much of high value and often difficult attainment in his life.

I recall a question posed to him by a reporter from a local newspaper at the end of an extensive interview. The reporter asked Dr. Wells what one thing he would have done differently if he could have the chance to re-create his administration. Dr. Wells looked out the window for such a long time, I wondered if he was going to find any answer. Finally and with some hesitation he answered, "Well, I suppose if I were to do it over again, I would put more money in the library collections."

I mentioned this reflection to Carl Jackson, former University Director of Libraries. Carl was astonished because, he said, "When I was at Iowa, we thought of Dr. Wells as the model university president for a university librarian to have because he paid so much attention to the needs of the library."

I imagine there were many struggling administrators at other universities who thought of Dr. Wells as an ideal administrator for advancing programs in their fields. I remember the remark of Dr. Clark Kerr in his first Patten Lecture at Indiana University that his search to find out what had caused I.U.'s rapid rise in academic respectability led to its secret weapon, Herman B Wells.

 DOTTIE COLLINS

The Source of His Memory

HERMAN Wells has often told me he remembers things that never happened. I don't really believe that, but I do know he has a phenomenal memory. As I have worked on hundreds of University ceremonies over the past ten years, I have called on that memory, and the Chancellor always steers me in the right direction and provides invaluable background information.

Recently, I prepared more than sixty-five letters for his signature. Though the letters were personalized, the content was essentially the same. Our office had attempted to verify the names and addresses, which had come from three different sources. I was somewhat taken aback when I saw that Chancellor Wells was going to read each name and address before he signed the letters.

From time to time as he went through the stack, he would make a comment or tell me a story about the person whose letter he was signing. At one point, he said, "She's dead!" and put the letter aside. "They are divorced," he said, reading another letter. "He lives in —— and she lives in ——." "He doesn't have a doctorate," he said about another. "Change that to Mr. and Mrs." He thought a moment and then added, "Well, he may have an honorary doctorate." Upon returning to my office, I set about to confirm this information. He was right on every count!

I am convinced his phenomenal memory is one of the chief

reasons Herman B Wells is such an eminent leader in higher education, a supporter of so many good causes, and a wonderful friend. I suspect that his extraordinary powers of recollection reflect the very high regard he has for his fellow human beings. He remembers people because he values them.

❖ W A Y N E   O .   C R A I G

"I'll Make You a Deal"

IN the fall of 1940, I.U.'s football team was struggling. Halfway through its schedule, the team was winless. Bill Menke, Bill Armstrong, and I made a decision to arouse the student body in an effort to support the football team in the homecoming game with the University of Iowa. The three of us went in different directions, personally visiting all the Greek organizations and dormitories on campus.

Our objective was to persuade the entire campus to mount pep rallies, join in snake dances through the campus and downtown Bloomington, and have constant chanting occurring on the way to classes to the tune of "Beat Iowa."

In our enthusiasm to gain student support, we bargained with students that a win over Iowa would mean no classes the following Monday. Needless to say, the "carrot" of Monday without classes persuaded the entire student enrollment of just under 5,000 students to help the team beat Iowa. The campus literally burst with an ongoing pep rally.

Iowa was leading the Big Ten at the time. They came to Bloomington to play the Hoosiers under the leadership of an All American quarterback named Nile Kinnick. Iowa was favored to win by 3 to 4 touchdowns. The combination of a fired-up team and a loud and supportive student body throughout the game resulted in a clear upset win for Indiana, 10–6.

On Sunday afternoon, President Wells was receiving phone calls from students inquiring whether or not there would be classes on Monday as a result of the "big game" victory. It was while receiving these phone calls that he learned that the three of us had made such a commitment to the student body.

President Wells called the three of us and requested that we come to his office. The net result of the meeting with President Wells was a compromise. As we all know, President Wells was a students' president. He showed his empathy for the great effort the student body had made in helping the team beat Iowa.

He said to the three of us, "I'll make you a deal," that classes would be held as scheduled on Monday, but in a show of his appreciation to the student body for the part they played in helping the team beat Iowa, he agreed to no classes on Monday after the Purdue game, providing Indiana won the game.

Needless to say, President Wells saved our necks with the students in making the Purdue offer. We were successful in keeping our credibility with the vast majority of the student body; they accepted the deal and proceeded to help the team prepare for, and defeat, Purdue, 3–0. And, yes, President Wells kept his word and officially called off classes on Monday following the Indiana victory over Purdue!

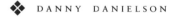 DANNY DANIELSON

A Wells Welcome

WITHIN a few weeks after I joined the faculty here in 1940 as Assistant Professor of Chemistry, I had a very encouraging experience involving then President Wells. My office, in the chemistry building, was at the east end of the corridor on the fourth floor. Fairly late in the afternoon of a warm Friday in September I was working at my desk, with the office door open. After a while I heard voices and the footsteps of men approaching my room from the open stairway some distance away. The two soon appeared at the door and I quickly invited them to enter. It was the robust President accompanied by the President of the Board of Trustees, Ora L. Wildermuth. After the meeting of the Trustees had adjourned, these two most responsible persons in the University had walked from Bryan Hall to the chemistry building and then ascended the 96 steps of the stairway to reach my office. The young President desired to introduce me to Mr. Wildermuth, and the two wanted to inquire about any unfilled needs I might have in beginning my professional life at Indiana University.

What a favorable beginning that was for me! I do not know to what degree the President exerted himself to welcome other new faculty and inquire about their needs. For me, it made a lasting impression. I had only met the President once and that was briefly in his office several months before when I had been invited to the campus prior to my appointment.

Like innumerable other faculty, alumni, and friends of the University, I am delighted that H. B Wells, over so many decades, has continued to represent the University superbly in wisdom, wit, and willingness to serve good causes. May this continue a long time.

❖ HARRY G. DAY

Kool-Aid

MY husband, Lyle Dieterle, was in the I.U. hospital under the care of Dr. James O. Ritchey, who was adjusting his insulin dose. Herman chanced to call and asked Lyle how he was doing. Lyle complained, "Herman, they're making me drink Kool-Aid." Herman drove to Indianapolis with real food, but Dr. Ritchey confiscated it. Both my husband and Herman survived.

Eagle Scout

WHEN our son, D. Paul Dieterle, was 16 he was made an Eagle Scout. The scouts were to run the city of Bloomington for a day. Tim Lemon became Mayor of Bloomington under the direction of Tom Lemon. Paul became President of Indiana University and reported for duty at 9:00 a.m. President Wells received him graciously, asked him what his interests were, and found that Paul liked to make jewelry. He produced some trays of inexpensive gems. Paul looked at all of them. Dr. Wells took him out to lunch, let him dictate a letter, and entertained him the entire day. When Paul returned home he said, "Dr. Wells is the most charming man I ever met. I wonder some girl didn't catch him." Herman's reply was, "Paul, I ran too fast."

Entitled to One Mistake

I was talking to Dr. Wells at the first fall entertainment at Showalter House. Herman and I sat together. Many people, of course, came up to speak to him. I said, "Herman, do you remember you hired Lyle in 1935?" Herman said, "Everyone is entitled to one mistake."

 MARY PAUL DIETERLE

17

The Hallmark of the Genius

IN the early months of 1987, when I was being considered for the presidency of Indiana University, I received a call from the President of the Board of Trustees, Dick Stoner. The University Chancellor, Herman B Wells, would be visiting in Philadelphia en route from Indiana to Florida, Mr. Stoner said, and would enjoy visiting with me. It does not take much knowledge of geography to realize that Philadelphia is somewhat of a detour on a path between Indiana and Florida, so I realized that it was an exaggeration to suggest that Chancellor Wells would be stopping in Philadelphia in the natural course of things. But I was thrilled. For decades I had read about this great man of higher education, one of the two or three most important American educators in our century.

We visited together for much of the afternoon, in my office at the University of Pennsylvania, where I was Provost. Dr. Wells began by telling me that he had not been on the Penn campus since he had come to help celebrate the University's bicentennial. Since we were then in the process of organizing the 250th celebration, I began to gain some sense of the remarkable reach back through time of Chancellor Wells. When I said that to him, he replied with a story. He remembered that when he was a student at Indiana University one of his teachers, then an emeritus faculty member, told of one of his elderly teachers who in turn had a teacher in the time of George Washington. Chancellor Wells laughed as he told the story and said that he had told it so many times that he had begun to think that he himself had taught George Washington.

Since coming to Indiana University, of course, I have learned much more about the extraordinary man whom we honor in this volume. He does have an incredible sense of where we have been. But it is his vision of the future that is the hallmark of his genius. All through the early years of his presidency, he kept in his desk plans of how the University could and should develop physically and academically, and he presided over the realization of those plans as the years went on. He reached out around the world with I.U. international programs that make our University better known in some parts of Asia and Europe than it is in our own country. He worked closely with private as well as public institutions of higher education for the benefit of the entire state. Most visibly, he understood the importance of a splendid environment and ensured that as the Bloomington campus grew it would retain its natural beauty, its architectural coherence, and the cohesiveness of a small campus.

It is a unique privilege to follow in Chancellor Wells' footsteps. He took giant strides and I cannot possibly keep up. But the strength, humor, and extraordinary insight that mark his character make it fun to try. For Ellen and for me, he is a special friend, and we salute him.

 TOM EHRLICH

King Arthur and St. George

IN his quiet way, Dr. Wells has long been one of the most influential men in the country, and as for all really great men, life seemed to have for him a certain basic simplicity. There was nothing complicated about devotion to duty; there was nothing mysterious about trying his best. Loyalty to country and leaders had no possible alternative.

I never heard him say any of these things, but his message was pretty clear to everyone. I am unable to tell whether he is more like a King Arthur who sent his alumni out on quests for I.U., or a St. George who captured the dragon and put him to work for I.U. It must be one or the other.

 BYRON K. ELLIOTT

A Trip to the Doctor

LATE one afternoon in the late 1970s Dr. Wells called me to say he had not been feeling well and had gone to the doctor without an appointment. I could tell he was a bit out of sorts.

He said that first of all he had to wait an hour in the doctor's office, but all was not lost because he had been able to take a nap for about forty-five minutes. Finally he was called in and a new young doctor examined him.

Following this, the doctor said he couldn't find anything specifically wrong, and Dr. Wells allowed that this was helpful. The doctor then inquired about his medicines and determined that he should reduce the medicines, which Dr. Wells related was even more helpful.

The doctor then suggested that nothing was wrong that losing forty pounds or so wouldn't help. Dr. Wells said, "Don't you know that was even more helpful." Then Dr. Wells protested, "He even charged me to tell me that!"

On Vanity

JANNETTE and I were at a meeting out of town with Dr. Wells, and we had gone to dinner one evening. While walking back to Dr. Wells' room, we discovered the cuff of his trousers had been undone. He asked Jannette if she could sew and if so could she repair the cuff. She replied that, of course, she could and would.

While she was repairing the cuff we were having a brief discussion particularly about clothing fashions and styles. Dr. Wells commented that he had all his suits, shirts, and so forth, tailored. We went on visiting and I could tell something was concerning him. About five minutes later he said, "I mentioned that I have my clothes tailored, but you know, it's not because I'm vain, but because I'm so misshapen."

Mr. President!

I have had the privilege to travel with Dr. Wells on many occasions, both here in Indiana and around the country. One day on a trip to Indianapolis, Dr. Wells was sharing with me the manuscript of a chapter of his book, *Being Lucky*, which he was then writing. It was a chapter about the early years of his presidency.

I commented about how there must have been differences in being Acting President, President, and Interim President. He looked straight at me and said rather pointedly, "You should understand that I was never Acting President, I was always the President."

❖ JAMES M. ELLIOTT

Tell It Like It Isn't

ALL of us know Herman's ability to seize the moment. The fond memory I have of him in this regard goes back many years to a simpler time in the University's existence when the deans of men and women (there may have been no such thing as a Dean of Students in that time) racked their brains each semester to figure how to hold students on the campus over weekends. One of their schemes was something that would not catch the attention of present-day student sophisticates, which was called a Fun Frolic. It consisted of a series of booths, in which, old-style carnival fashion, the frats and sororities and any other group feeling the spirit could have something going, perhaps for the sum of twenty-five cents. Piotr Wandycz, then my office mate, now a distinguished professor at Yale, and I, both being single, went over and spent some time throwing custard pies at coeds. But as we were passing down a dark aisle I saw one of the old-fashioned huge scales and a bulky, unmistakable figure standing beside it. The figure was concentrating on a customer, a thin little girl who was standing on the scale. If she weighed anything, she weighed ninety-five pounds, maybe ninety-six. Herman took a look at her, frowned, looked again, and yelled out, "One hundred and twenty-five!" As Piotr and I watched, fascinated, the girl stepped off the scale triumphantly, Herman shook his head sadly, and then he presented her with a big doll, her prize. The girl had paid twenty-five cents to be weighed. The doll, I suppose, was worth fifty cents.

 ROBERT H. FERRELL

Mr. Manners

IN the old Memorial Stadium, the front two rows were called boxes. They consisted of a metal railing separating every four seats. My mother sat on the front row of our box next to the railing where Dr. Wells' mother was seated in his box. They would spend the afternoon talking of things other than football while, right behind them, my father and Dr. Wells would use a good amount of the time conducting University business—the President being interrupted often by friends and alumni wanting to say hello.

As a young boy, I had little interest in any of those conversations and, being seated too low in the stadium to see over the players standing on the sideline, my main interest lay in the concessionaires selling their wares. After I convinced my mother to buy popcorn, she gave the usual reminder to share with others. I grudgingly made an offer to my sister, my mother, and finally, to my father, who was intently listening to the President. Without changing expression, Dr. Wells leaned over and looked at me and said, "No thank you, J. A., I don't care for any either." My father glanced in my direction; but he said nothing—he didn't have to. I had just learned an important lesson in politeness.

❖   J .   A .   F R A N K L I N ,   J R .

Herman as Machiavelli

DR. Wells had some difficulty coming up with a structure and format for his autobiography, *Being Lucky*. It was partly a problem of too many advisers. Finally, in desperation, I gave him a copy of Machiavelli's *The Prince* and said, "Here, this is a model. Pretend you are Machiavelli telling the University world how you did it."

The Prince is a series of short essays offering harshly realistic— some might say cynical—advice on how to run a strong central government. My thinking was that the essay format, and the conversational tone, would provide a perfect model for Dr. Wells, who liked to write while he was on trips and in odd moments when time became available. Here was a format that would enable him to say how he did it without having to worry too much about the overall structure of the book.

My suggestion was a disaster. He stopped working on the book. What was aimed at freeing him of constraints instead froze the flow of manuscript. I managed eventually to get my advice canceled. More manuscript appeared. I was invited in for an editorial conference. I said I was reluctant to say anything because my last effort had had the opposite effect from what was intended. It was after lunch. We were sitting in Dr. Wells' Owen Hall office. He was behind the big conference table that dominates one side of the room. He was in a reflective mood, absorbed my comments, ruminated, and finally spoke. "Yes," he said, "I read that book you gave me. You're right. I was like that. But I can't write that kind of book."

What could he have told us if he were not a Victorian gentleman?

Vodka

AT a crowded reception, I asked Dr. Wells if I could get him a drink from the bar.

"Yes," he said. "Vodka on the rocks."

When I returned, he thanked me and confided, "I always drink vodka. It won't give you a hangover and no one can smell it on your breath."

 JOHN GALLMAN

The Wells Touch

LATE one hot summer afternoon I found myself crammed into a window seat at the back of a 727 jetliner at New York's LaGuardia Airport awaiting departure to Louisville.

The last passenger in was Dr. Wells. He came down the long aisle and plopped down next to me. He said not a word and promptly went to sleep.

An hour or so later he woke up with a snort, turned to me and said, "George, the older you get the more you look like your father."

This happened at least 15 years after my graduation from I.U.

and I had not seen Dr. Wells in the interim. He had indeed been a friend of my father's, but hadn't seen him for many years.

The nap? He explained that a heavy lunch and spirits at his favorite oyster bar in New York had temporarily dulled his alertness.

❖   G E O R G E   N .   G I L L

The Value of Luxury

WHEN I was a freshman in the fall of 1938, Herman Wells devoted one afternoon a week to visit with students. I remember vividly the time I took advantage of this opportunity. I had just pledged Theta and was enjoying living in the then "new" house. I expressed my great satisfaction with the luxury of the living conditions. Dr. Wells said he believed it was important to give students the highest possible standard of living because it would be a measure they would strive to maintain or surpass. The Greek system is alive and well on the Indiana campus largely due to the support and wisdom of this man.

❖   M A R Y   R E E S   G I L L I A T T

Leadership and Love

MY good fortune to get to know Herman B Wells started in 1970 when I began law school at I.U. Bloomington. I had a part-time job working with Paul Klinge, who was then the able right-hand man for both President Ryan and Chancellor Wells. I, like Paul, split my duties between Bryan and Owen Halls.

Of course, during my undergraduate days, I had heard of the immense stature of Dr. Wells at Indiana University. I had even met him a couple of times but did not get to know him or see him operate.

There are several experiences I had with Dr. Wells which I will forever remember: they help illustrate why he is a living legend, why he has meant so much to Indiana University and thousands of Indiana University alumni and friends, and his incredible leadership abilities.

I had very limited duties for Dr. Wells in my part-time job. Occasionally he would ask me to write letters of acknowledgment or appreciation to various Indiana University students and faculty members for his signature. It was his way of keeping in touch with people, thanking them for their contributions to Indiana University and generally letting them know they were important and their achievements were at least noted by him. I remember to this day getting a real high from Dr. Wells with his compliment on the draft letter to Mark Spitz. Mark had done something outstanding (pre-seven Olympic gold medals), and Dr. Wells asked that he be recognized. Dr. Wells gave Mark and me a leadership lesson with that experience.

I also enjoyed seeing the meticulous care in which Dr. Wells worked at developing and maintaining relationships with people. By way of illustration, he would time his walks from Owen Hall to other campus locations when students were traveling from class to class so that he and the students would have an opportunity to have exposure to each other. He would also keep notes of, for example, dinner meetings with "friends" of Indiana University so that he could later drop them a note or plan a subsequent dinner with their favorite flower setting or course selection in mind. He was effective, and it was not the result of happenstance.

One saying about Dr. Wells I picked up early on was that "Indiana University was his sole mistress." I believe that is true, and we are all beneficiaries of it.

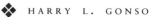 HARRY L. GONSO

Senior class picture, Lebanon
High School, 1920.

The very young Wells with his
father, Granville Wells, 1903.

First official portrait as
President of Indiana
University, 1938.
(*Harris and Ewing*)

President Wells and Coach Bo
McMillan celebrate I.U.'s first
Big Ten football championship,
1945. (*Allan Grant*)

On appointment in 1947 as
Special Advisor on Cultural
Affairs to the Military
Governor, Office of Military
Government for Germany
(U.S.).

Signing the diplomas of the graduating class of 1949.

With former President
William Lowe Bryan,
1950.

With John Foster Dulles,
1955.

Paul Weatherwax presents a cake from the Faculty Council on
the twentieth anniversary of the Wells presidency, 1957.

Passing the torch to Elvis J. Stahr, President of Indiana
University, 1962–1968.

Chancellor Wells with his mother,
Mrs. Granville Wells, 1964.

Bundled up for the chilly weather during a
Little 500 race in the 1970s.

Playing Santa Claus, a favorite I.U.
Christmastime tradition, 1970s.

With John W. Ryan,
President of Indiana
University, 1971–1987.

Celebrating at the Gables
on Hoagy Charmichael's
75th birthday, 1974.
(*David Jay*)

Walking through campus, 1978.

Class of 1924 member of
the Emeritus Club, 1970s.

Wells reads Wells—*Being
Lucky,* published by
the Indiana University
Press, 1980.

Chancellor Herman B Wells and President Thomas Ehrlich
pose beneath a portrait of Indiana University's first president,
Andrew Wylie, 1990. (© *1992 Garrett Ewald*)

The Personal Touch

WHEN I accepted a position in Bryan Hall during the early 1960s, I was told by my associates that President Wells knew everyone in the building by their first name, from custodians to clericals to vice presidents. I must admit I was skeptical, but quickly learned that he not only knew the employees, he also knew of their families. If there was a sick child or parent, President Wells was among the first to inquire about their progress; if there was a death, he personally delivered his condolences. He joined the staff members in their triumphs—a scholarship won, a successful athletic contest, a marriage, a new baby . . . He was never too busy to acknowledge a job well done, or to express appreciation for extra effort.

I remained in Bryan Hall only four years, but yet today when I see Chancellor Wells, he makes me feel as though he clearly remembers me from those days some thirty years ago.

 ROSANN R. GREENE

Small Town Touch

SEVERAL summers ago, Chancellor Wells called me one afternoon to ask if I had time to see him for a few minutes. He had two things on his mind. The first came to him after he went to the funeral of an old friend—he was doing that a lot these days, he said—and then spent time being driven around small towns in western Indiana. In almost each town, he remembered some young man or woman who graduated from a small school in that town, came to I.U., and then returned to become president of the local bank, principal or superintendent of schools, president of the Chamber of Commerce, editor of the local newspaper. He was struck by how many of the small schools had closed and how many of the students from these small towns were now going to large consolidated schools. What concerned him was that I.U. might be missing some of these bright young people who were still being raised in small Indiana towns. He asked if it were possible to find out how many current students came from Indiana towns with populations under 2,000. It seemed to me extraordinary that, nearly a quarter of a century after his active involvement in university administration, he still was concerned about the meaning and significance of a public university and worrying about whether the sophistication of I.U.'s recruiting efforts was passing by those bright young people like the ones he remembered who had done so much to enhance the life of their communities when they returned home after attending I.U. How many of us worry about such things?

IVY Tech

CHANCELLOR Wells had seen an ad in the local paper for IVY Tech's schedule of classes for the fall and had called for one. He was interested not only in what was being offered, but also in the cost of attending the courses. As he said to me, the intention of the creation of IVY Tech—and he was much involved in it—was to make it possible for someone who wanted to be a plumber to be the best possible plumber, for someone who wanted to be a carpenter to be the best possible carpenter, and so on. It mattered to him that IVY Tech limit course offerings to its noble mission, and also offer them at prices that would make it possible for all people to attend. As with his concern about the young people from small towns, it was striking to me that of all people in Bloomington, Herman Wells would call to request IVY Tech's schedule of classes, and then review it closely with the concerns he expressed to me in mind. How many of us, especially those in higher education, worry about these matters?

Forever Wells

SEVERAL years ago, at an alumni barbecue, Chancellor Wells spoke about a meeting he had with Indiana's oldest living citizen. Somehow, during his description, it turned out that the oldest living citizen had a grandparent who had attended Indiana University and whose parent had been given land as a gift resulting from his close association during the Revolutionary War with George Washington. After awhile, either because of the heat or because of Wells' story-telling skills, it became unclear to me whether the oldest citizen was somehow in touch with our nation's first president or whether Wells himself had spoken to George Washington. Either way, it suggested a remarkable continuity that opened up, historically and personally, our university.

Shortly later, it was my privilege to preside over a smaller ceremony—perhaps 30 people were there. That was the restoration of the Centennial Steps and Memorial Pillar in Dunn Meadow. The individual who had donated funds to renovate the area had died the previous fall, but his daughter was there, a 1960 I.U. graduate, with two of his granddaughters, one a 1988 I.U. graduate. His daughter noted that in 1928 when her father was a sophomore on this campus, he had as one of his faculty members a brash young business professor named Herman B Wells. She noted that, thirty-two years later, when she graduated in 1960, she received her degree from the President of the University, Herman B Wells. And on that day sixty years later when her own daughter received her undergraduate degree, the Commencement speaker was Herman B Wells.

 KEN GROS LOUIS

"The Bottom of a Bird Cage"

I had just started working with the I.U. Foundation Board of Directors and we were meeting out of town. Dr. Wells had missed our dinner the evening before the first session because he did not feel well. When he came into the meeting early the next morning, I went over to check on him. I said I was sorry he did not feel well the evening before and asked, "How are you feeling this morning?" His reply: "Like the bottom of a bird cage."

❖ CAROL S. GROSS

Faculty Consensus

DURING the first years of Herman's administration, the Faculty Council, or anything like it, did not exist. Instead, the faculty voice was heard through general faculty meetings involving all who would attend. One such meeting, like many, dragged on for hours, mired down in tiresome discussion of procedural matters, and adjourned without a decision on any item on the agenda.

As we walked back from the meeting I said to Herman, "I'll bet the faculty wouldn't agree on anything but a pay raise!" He replied, "Don't be too sure they'd agree on that!"

The Governor's Daughter

ONE day, during the first week in September, the phone rang and Herman said, "Charlie, Governor Gates just called and wants to know why his daughter, Patty, has to be down here for registration a whole week before classes begin." I answered, "She doesn't. I expect she's down here because this is sorority rush week and she's Rush Chairman over at the Theta House." "Ho. Ho. Wait 'til I tell him," Herman chuckled. "I'll let you know." Soon he called back: "Charlie, the Governor said 'Oh Damn! Sorry I bothered you. And that's why she had all those girls at the Governor's Mansion this summer.' "

 CHARLES HARRELL

The Right Age

WHEN I was interviewed for the deanship of the I.U. School of Dentistry, President Wells asked me if I thought I could handle the deanship. I answered that although I had had very little experience in administration, I would certainly like to try. Chancellor Wells replied that he knew of a man my age (38) who was appointed president of a large university, and apparently was successful. I didn't know until much later that he was referring to himself.

Mother Knows Best

SEVERAL years ago I was riding in the back seat of Dr. Wells' car with his mother. Dr. Wells (I could never bring myself to call him Herman) was sitting in the front seat with his driver when he had to use his handkerchief. Mrs. Wells said sternly, "Herman, you should always use a clean handkerchief!"

No News Is Good News

A few months after I assumed the deanship of the School of Dentistry, I realized I hadn't seen Dr. Wells for some time, so I told him I was worried because he hadn't called or visited me. He replied, "You shouldn't worry *until* I start to come around."

❖ MAYNARD K. HINE

In the Pool

It was the summer of 1949, and we were both students in summer school in Bloomington. Brown County State Park had opened its beautiful pool, and thoughts of the coolness and the setting were magnets. Crowds of people were there, a happy mass of Hoosiers—and there, too, was President Wells, swimming merrily away. It delighted us to have him with us in the pool, a complete surprise at first and then a warm feeling of "family." It was, and is, the essence of this great man: we know he is "in the pool" with all of us.

❖ HARRIETT AND DICK INSKEEP

The Little Jeep That Couldn't

My first trip to Bradford Woods in the early 1950s was an adventure. Dr. John D. Van Nuys, Dean of the I.U. School of Medicine, invited me, then an Instructor in Medicine, to join him on a trip to see the woods which had recently become the property of Indiana University. At the site we met President Herman B Wells and Rey Carlson of HPER. We left the Manor House in an old jeep with Dr. Wells in the front, and Van Nuys (considerably corpulent) and Irwin in the back seat. We started up the steep hill on a dirt road and the jeep stalled about halfway on this climb. Fortunately the brakes worked and Rey backed safely down the hill. Van Nuys and Irwin got out and then pushed the vehicle and its two occupants to the top. As I recall, Dr. Wells' comment was "That *was* a rather hairy trip."

 GLENN W. IRWIN, JR.

The Starter

AFTER I graduated from I.U. I practiced law at Fort Wayne and as a result became a very good friend of Bill Kunkle, who was then on the Board of Trustees and ran the Fort Wayne *Journal Gazette* newspaper. On one occasion, Herman Wells joined us at the *Journal Gazette* for lunch. Bill Kunkle mentioned to Herman, who was then on his way to Europe, "Herman, you start all these new buildings, and then you leave town and leave the work of completing the building to us." Herman replied, "Well, I at least get them started and all of you fellows ought to be able to finish it."

❖ PAUL G. JASPER

Weekend Guests

IT was a bright Saturday morning in October and the lobby of the Indiana Memorial Union Building was bursting with people who were attempting to check into their rooms before going to the football game. The long line at the check-in desk was not moving too fast! The nervous young desk clerk kept explaining to a well-dressed elderly gentleman at the head of the line that pets were not allowed in the overnight rooms.

The man, not knowing what to do with his little dog, was using all of his abilities to put pressure on the clerk. He repeated several times in a loud voice that President Wells was his long-time friend and former roommate. The clerk had his orders and was not moved. Other persons in line kept looking at their watches.

At this instant Herman Wells entered the lobby, his gait indicating that he was late for whatever meeting he was trying to attend. The elderly gentleman in question spied him and moved quickly to intercept Dr. Wells.

After hearing the sad plight of the alumnus and former roommate, Dr. Wells replied without batting an eye that the desk clerk did have his orders, but more importantly he wanted to visit with his old crony and invited him and his wife (and dog) to stay with him at the President's house for the weekend.

The elderly gentleman was delighted and rounded up his wife and dog and headed for Bryan House. President Wells proceeded to his appointment and some lucky alumnus on the waiting list received a room at the Union.

Do You Remember Me?

FOR people who have the public eye, the comment they most hate to hear is: "Do you remember me?"

To those of us who have been privileged to work with Dr. Wells it comes as no surprise that literally thousands of people have commented that "Herman Wells remembered me." Perhaps the most notable trait that the man possesses is his ability to recognize uncountable numbers of people who have crossed his path through life. Furthermore, his gigantic memory seems to be able to place these people in the proper perspective as to who they are and where they live and work. He also remembers a wide range of persons from hotel clerks to legislators.

How in the world does he do it? By working at it! From notes quickly scratched out and shoved in a coat pocket to brushing up on a list of names he has accumulated while he is en route to a meeting on land, sea, or air.

Herman Wells definitely is a candidate for being the champion funeral attender. He has attended thousands of funerals! Typically while on the road to a funeral he will open a conversation with his fellow passengers on the subject of who, besides the family of the deceased, will be there. Names of these possible attendees are spoken and noted and Herman Wells will definitely be ready by the time he arrives.

Sure, he has a great memory! But more importantly he works at remembering people at all levels. The records he has amassed are accurate and up-to-date. They are important to him and he studies them continuously.

Who was it that said: genius is one percent inspiration and 99 percent perspiration? I don't know, I forget!

 FRANK B. JONES

The Memory of an Elephant

WHEN I was graduate from college (not I.U.), Herman Wells was the commencement speaker. I happened to be first in the "line of march" and was introduced to then President Wells. Time passed and a few years later as a graduate student (this time at I.U.), I was invited to a garden party at the Wells home. When I presented myself in the receiving line, President Wells remembered not only my name, but also the circumstances of our first meeting.

Since I joined the I.U.P.U.–Fort Wayne faculty I have had many occasions to speak with Herman Wells and he never forgets. Indiana University will also never forget the contributions of Herman Wells.

❖ JOANNE B. LANTZ

The Forgotten Desk

IN Herman's early professional years he loved collecting antique furniture. One of the beautiful shops he often visited was in Danville, Kentucky. Returning to the shop after an absence of several years and deep into his very busy life as President of Indiana University, he saw a desk which he much admired. He decided to buy the desk for his home in Woodburn House. Imagine his surprise when the owner of the shop said, "Why, Dr. Wells, you already own it; the desk is yours. You paid for it when you visited us four years ago. You were to let us know when you wanted it delivered to Bloomington."

❖ ELEANOR R. LONG

Choosing a Dean

SOON after Wells became President, the University inaugurated compulsory retirement at age 70 for faculty and administrators.

Among the large number retired at that time was Winfred B. Merrill, Dean of the School of Music.

When Wells had narrowed the number of applicants for the music deanship vacancy to two, he arranged for the two to visit the campus a week or so apart. For each of them he held a luncheon meeting with the music faculty, which then numbered only nine. As I recall, Wells did not attend the luncheons, but after the music faculty had visited with both candidates, he invited the faculty members to come one at a time to his office, where he questioned each one as to his or her preference and the reasons for the choice.

With support from the faculty thus interviewed, Robert L. Sanders was the candidate chosen. When Wells telephoned Sanders to offer him the deanship, Sanders warned Wells that after his visit to the campus he had shaved off his beard. Wells jokingly replied, "Well, that does put a new face on the matter."

Herman and Trees

HERMAN valued trees. He was distressed when all the trees along Kirkwood Avenue were cut down when he was out of town and could not protest.

When he learned one day that a handsome tree near Myers Hall might be cut down, he secured a comfortable chair and sat in it all day beneath the tree to make sure the tree was saved. The tree is still there and an access road was built around it.

I didn't witness his vigil to save the tree, but have heard the story often.

❖ NEWELL H. LONG

All's Wells That Ends Well

In 1938 the Longs wrote their first faculty fun show, *Inaugurating the Boy President*, to greet the newly appointed Herman B Wells, the youngest college president in the country. Following is a song from the play:

BE YOURSELF

Be yourself, just be yourself;
Be yourself from day to day.
Be yourself, just be yourself;
That's the Herman B Wells way.
He avoids all ostentation,
No pretense or affectation;
He's a pleasant, humble, normal, friendly one.
He assumes no pose to please,
He has natural poise and ease,
Genuine, sincere, and honest, loving fun.
All these things endear the man;
Emulate him if you can.
Be yourself, just be yourself;
That's the Herman B Wells way.

 SONG AND LYRICS BY NEWELL H. LONG

Travel

In the middle '70s Herman was one of a number of I.U. alumni on a cruise in the Mediterranean, which commenced in Dubrovnik and ended at the Port of Rome. During the cruise we ran into some bad weather, as well as uncleanliness of the ship. Herman's great comment, which applied to all travelers, was:

"If a traveler expects the comfort of home, he should stay there."

❖ ROBERT A. LUCAS

Corn Squeezings

THE adventures of driving an open touring car as a very young chauffeur for his amiable grandfather were described fondly by Herman Wells fifty years later. This became suspenseful when the driving was into the hills of Kentucky, where relatives insisted upon making generous gifts of hams, fruits, and garden produce as well as the local "corn squeezings," Prohibition notwithstanding.

Particularly after crossing the Ohio River on the way home, young Herman would drive in the most law-abiding manner possible, with close attention to hazards which could cause a flat tire, hoping fervently that nothing would interfere with the safe delivery of the contraband cargo and a completely relaxed grandfather, who saw no problem with gifts from relatives.

❖ DOROTHY MCCREA

Thin Onions

ON one occasion the dinner included generous slices of Bermuda onions, which Dr. Wells liked. Mrs. Wells was always concerned about Dr. Wells eating foods that didn't agree with him or that might not be appropriate before going out for the evening. Bermuda onions seemed to fit both of those categories. Mrs. Shields had instructions about such foods, but she often found it convenient to "forget." Mrs. Wells was, of course, served first, but she did not comment on the onions. Then as I approached Dr. Wells with the serving tray, she said, "Now Herman, you know you're not supposed to eat those onions. And besides, we're going out tonight." His deft reply is a tribute to this man's success as a formidable debater: "These are all right, Mother. They're sliced thin." The logic of his response lasted at least long enough for the onions to be consumed!

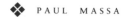

PAUL MASSA

Food, Food, Food

WE were in Lucerne on an alumni tour and had just dined elegantly in a beautiful restaurant by the lake. A string trio was playing a Viennese waltz and I said, "I could dance all night." Dr. Wells answered, "I could EAT all night!"

HANSI MENDEL

The Slow Fast Break

MY first social meeting with Dr. Herman B Wells was at Woodburn House after our I.U. team won the N.C.A.A. national basketball championship in 1940. In introducing the team, Herman obviously knew the regular players, but not the subs. When he got around to introducing the rinky-dinks, he did not hesitate or lose any of his usual savoir faire, simply asking each one to introduce himself. We felt no embarrassment and neither did he. It was a lesson I learned which served me well throughout life, and that was never to be upset when called upon to introduce persons whose names I could not remember.

As a Trustee of I.U. for six years, I observed Herman at many social functions. He was always very gracious, moving freely among crowds of people, shaking hands, making everyone feel that he was particularly delighted to meet each one. Some lesser leaders in the family of the University have never achieved such politesse. They have been observed to look over shoulders of loquacious interlocutors to see who more important politically might be coming next.

Herman could also be a little crafty. To use an oxymoron, he enjoyed a slow fast break at cocktail parties, never drinking, appearing to enjoy many superficial conversations. But all the time he was well aware of the location of exit doors and headed inexorably in the right direction. It has been said that he planned his strategy well in advance and over the years learned the location of every back door of every faculty house on the campus.

I cannot vouch for all the Wells mythopoeia, even though I did live on the campus for three years. One story has it that Herman carried binocular eyeglasses and a card in his shirt pocket secured by one of his suspenders. When a legislator was in the same room, Herman would slip on the glasses, and, as he appeared to be glancing at the card, he would scan name tags dead ahead. He has always known that every politician likes to be called by his first name!

 ROBERT H. MENKE

The Hot Tub Overfloweth

I have many fond remembrances as an undergraduate, alumnus, and I.U. Foundation Board member. However, one of the most vivid in my memory took place a few years ago at the Ocean Reef Club in Florida during a Foundation Board meeting.

Dr. Wells joined me in the hot tub adjacent to the swimming pool and, with the two of us, the tub overflowed and no one ventured to join us. The capacity of the tub was exceeded; however, the conversation was delightful. I have a picture commemorating this momentous occasion.

❖ THOMAS M. MILLER

Watermelon Education

THE first time I met Dr. Wells was at a book signing in the Student Union, where he was autographing copies of his book, *Being Lucky*. As I waited in line I thought to myself: if Indiana University had a pair of legs, then this is the body that would provide the driving force. Once I was in place to have my copy signed I handed over my slightly perspiration-moistened text. Dr. Wells asked me where I was from and I replied "Jackson County." He asked if I meant Jackson County, Indiana. When I said yes he proceeded to list the leading virtues of my home: "fertile farmland, a great county fair, and as far as I know, the best damn watermelons anywhere in the world!" As I stood there I was given a quick lesson in understanding dichotomies and the advantages of a broad-based education.

❖ TROY MURRAY-PLUMER

Sundays in the Woods

IT was sixty years ago when I was brought quietly into the circle of friendship that surrounded Herman B Wells. I was not taking courses in the Business School, where he was an Assistant Professor, so I am not aware of just how I was recognized.

I was working on *The Daily Student*—where you learned quickly there was no period after the B! Also I had been elected to the Union Board, to which Herman had been elected when he was an undergraduate.

Whatever the reason, Herman included me with four other juniors or seniors in a group that had no name nor any reason for being except to be gathered together on Sunday afternoons in the spring for "wordly" discussions. The beginning was rather striking for a group of country boys.

Herman would drive up to our various houses in his awesome silver and maroon Packard touring car—with the top down—and we would settle in for the drive out East Third Street. When we reached a place that Herman judged appropriate, maybe still in Monroe County or possibly in Brown County, he would turn off the dusty road for us to gather in a grassy plot well into the trees away from prying eyes.

Once settled, the brew would be uncorked and we would all sip slowly while Herman nudged us into discussions of wide and varied interests. What an opportunity to have the challenge of education provided by a mind that the entire world would recognize and honor a few short years later! We probably were too naive to be impressed at that time, but the memories have provided a background that has helped me accomplish much of whatever I did in a lifetime.

As the sun began to sink into the West, we would settle into that beautiful Packard and journey back into the community that was Indiana University and its campus.

Thanks to Herman B Wells, our true education began sixty years ago!

❖ ROBERT C. PEBWORTH

Only His Mother

DOTI and I arrived at the Little Theatre for an evening production at the same time as Herman and his mother. In approaching the usher who requested tickets, I overheard Mrs. Wells say as she pointed back toward Herman, "I am with the fat boy."

Just Dessert

HAVING just completed a gourmet meal, Herman moved back from the table and patting his stomach contentedly he said, "One could say I have not missed too many meals."

Always expressing a fondness for desserts, I recall Herman once saying after a rich dessert that one works himself through the course of the meal just to get to the most important part of the meal—the dessert!

 RUDY POZZATTI

The People's Choice

THE legends of Herman Wells are authenticated by the record of his many accomplishments, and mean many things to many people. His early dedication and devotion to Indiana University was an indication of things to come. I have known him all my life and during his student days on this campus spent many hours listening to him tell me, a high school student, about the "Glory of Old I.U." That dedication has never changed.

The often told story of how he was chosen as Acting President of the University is a true one. Dr. William Lowe Bryan had announced his resignation as President, effective July 1, 1937. The Trustees spent two years looking for a successor but one week before the deadline had not made a decision. They decided to appoint an Acting President for an interim period, thereby giving them more time. Herman B Wells, then Dean of the School of Business, was chosen for that position.

Judge Ora L. Wildermuth, President of the Trustees, called Herman at 2:00 a.m. that night to inform him and get his consent. Herman protested and suggested there were other deans with longer tenure and more experience who should be considered. Judge Wildermuth replied, "The reason we are asking you to do this is because you are the only dean who will not be considered for the presidency." After a few months, they re-examined their qualifications list and realized that the man sitting in the President's chair was the only one meeting all of their requirements.

Rich Reward

DURING the 1950s, President Wells proposed the University create a prestigious award to be conferred upon alumni "to provide recognition for outstanding achievements benefiting their community, state, nation or university." This became the Distinguished Alumni Service Award and was identified as "the highest award given by the University for which alumni *only* are eligible."

The Trustees enthusiastically approved the idea and I was asked to submit a plan for the selection of the recipients. The assignment took some time to research, coordinate suggestions, and finalize, so a few weeks went by without my report. One day Herman and I were talking to a Trustee who was concerned about my tardiness and so indicated. Finally, Herman said, "Don't worry about it. He will get it done. It just takes him longer than some people."

I.U. Forever

DURING my tenure as University Liaison Officer to the State House and Legislature, it was not unusual to get aggravated at one or more legislators because of their attitude toward Indiana University. Such was the case during one bad week, and I was still irritated during the report session in Bloomington on Saturday morning. Herman suggested I might be pushing the panic button too soon since "Legislators come and legislators go, but Indiana University goes on forever."

Mister Janitor

WHEN someone acquires a nickname as a youth, it is not unusual for his life-long friends to continue to use it in later years, regardless of status or position of the individual. Herman says there once was a janitor on the campus whom everyone called "Mr. ————." A distinguished foreign diplomat was visiting the campus and later remarked he couldn't understand the customs of American universities where everyone called the janitor "Mister" and the president "Hermie."

The Antique Hunter

ONE day I wandered into the Chancellor's office and he proposed we take a trip somewhere. When I asked him where he wanted to go, to my surprise he mentioned Kentucky and Tennessee to see the distilleries. I didn't know then that there are as many fine antique shops in that area as there are distilleries— all of which he knew about, some in which he was a customer, and most of which we visited.

One of the places on our itinerary was Lynchburg, Tennessee, home of the famous Jack Daniels Distillery. This is many miles from where we were in Kentucky. Thinking, for that reason, he might want to cancel the trip there, I asked him if he knew where it was located. He replied, "No, where?" When I told him he said, "So what?" That ended the conversation.

Guess what—there was an antique shop there he wanted to see . . .

 CLAUDE RICH

Always a Gambler

THERE was a remark about Herman that was popular when he was a student. It was reported with great amusement by students who considered it quite funny. The line went that Herman was president of the Y.M.C.A. on the campus and at the same time was the best poker player in school. It was a description that does not seem inconsistent or beyond propriety today, but in that day — some time in the twenties—it was titillating, if not a bit shocking. Such were the mores of the time that the thought of a Y.M.C.A. leader indulging in poker games smacked of a church elder frequenting gambling halls.

DOW RICHARDSON

A Good Book

I shall never forget the autumn of 1968 when Dr. Wells was Interim President from September through December. It was a tense time. Emotions ran high as students and faculty expressed many different views on such issues as *in loco parentis*, governance, research policy, R.O.T.C., campus recruitment activities (C.I.A., and so on), and through it all, the controversy over the U.S. participation in the Vietnam war.

In the welter of all the debate and demonstration, a fire was discovered late one afternoon in the Library, which at that time was located just north of Bryan Hall. I rushed from my office to see the extent of the fire (it was extinguished with minimal damage to the collection, unlike a "follow-up" fire a few days later which destroyed important parts of the collection, but that is another story). At the moment no one knew the cause of the fire, but as I stood next to HBW on the roadway, watching the smoke billow around the limestone figures and over the familiar inscription, "A Good Book Is the Precious Life-Blood of a Master Spirit," I saw tears course down his cheeks. I knew he feared that the fire evidenced an escalation in the confrontation tactics of the time. He could not restrain his distraught emotions—for the books themselves, the old library, the campus family, and the traditions of freedom but not license for the University.

Victory

DR. Wells faithfully follows the athletic teams of Indiana University. On occasions of victory he would say to me, "A good victory is great for the President!" and he was correct.

The Rose

ONE year after my election to the presidency, a rather contentious and stormy year, I received from Dr. Wells a single rose and a note which said, "Remember the beauty and perfume of the rose, not the momentary sting of its thorns."

Citizen of the World

WHEN I think of the international stature of Indiana University, I think of when Pat and I persuaded Dr. Wells to attend the quinquennial meeting of the International Association of Universities. He had been a founding President in the 1950s, and the meeting was to be held in Manila, where Indiana alumni are numerous and devoted. We arrived late at night, but nevertheless the airport was thronged with the I.U. reception group—easily in the hundreds of people of all ages, with banners and crimson hats and shirts everywhere. A few days later, the formal sessions of the meeting began, and I watched as Dr. Wells walked slowly down the center aisle, being greeted by delegates from every country. He knew some from the early days. All knew him from his reputation, and thus all knew of Indiana University. Finally, as he arrived at the place of the U.S. delegation, the delegates rose to give standing applause to one they recognized as a distinguished citizen of the world.

·

Catfish and Diets

HBW has a justly deserved reputation as a connoisseur of food— all kinds of food. But nothing gets his attention like fresh catfish. I remember getting a call from Dr. Wells on a summer afternoon in 1968 as follows: "I just heard that they have a fresh batch of catfish at the Country Club, and I want you and Pat to join me tonight for a catfish fry." We did, and it was delicious—and unforgettable.

Which reminds me of an occasion at Bryan House when we were having one of the innumerable cocktail receptions. Dr. Wells arrived early because, he said, he always enjoyed visiting a little while with Pat, and could only do so before guests started to arrive. Pat was busy with last minute preparations and finally found HBW moving around the hors d'oeuvre table sampling the food. Since Dr. Wells had recently been on a serious diet (including several weeks at Duke University), Pat sympathized and apologized for the great temptation of the many delectable dishes. Whereupon HBW responded, "Don't give it another thought; you know, the food you eat standing up doesn't count in a diet!"

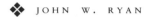 JOHN W. RYAN

A Piece of Cake

I am attending a student-faculty banquet, which concludes with a particularly luscious chocolate cake. There is only one slice left on the serving plate. I am sitting on Herman's right, calculating my chances of discreetly grabbing the leftover piece—but the boy sitting on his left reaches for it first. As fast as lightning, Wells slaps the student's wrist. He says, "Don't be so greedy, young man!" Then he eats the cake himself.

He Never Forgets a Name

INCHING forward in a reception line, my wife just ahead of me, we confront Dr. Wells. He grabs her hand, struggling to remember

who she is. So I say, "Mr. President, you remember my wife . . . "
"Of course I do," he says, "but her beauty so dazzles me, for a moment I forgot everything else."

Hard Ball

ONCE, in the 1960s, I received a strong outside offer, and was told by Ralph Collins (then Dean of Faculties) to go see HBW. The audience, in the President's office, went something like this:

HBW (looking disgruntled): So? Frank Murphy is after you, is he?
TAS: Yes, sir.
HBW: I see you're having lunch at the Tudor Room quite often.
TAS: That's so, sir.
HBW: And you know that I like to have lunch there too?
TAS: Yes, sir.
HBW: And you know I like to eat?
TAS: It is known, sir.
HBW: Do you realize that if I didn't see you at lunch it would spoil my appetite?
TAS: OK, I'll stay at I.U.

How to Handle Student Protests

DURING the days of student protests, a ragged group, to air a multitude of grievances and to excoriate Wells, gather on the grass between Bryan Hall and what is now Franklin Hall. I stand at the fringes of the congregation to watch how he handles this. An angry student leader, haranguing interminably, denounces the

President and reads a long litany of unnegotiable demands. Wells, cupping his ear, says softly, "Young man, I am so sorry, but I don't hear so well any more. Would you please repeat what you said?" The anger dissolves in laughter.

Advisor to the President

I am proud to be appointed a Presidential Consultant to plan for what will eventually become the Mathers Museum of World Cultures. I set forth, in some detail, my ideas to the committee chaired by Wells. He then presents, but more crisply, his own ideas, which are diametrically opposed to mine. I feel discouraged, until he winds up, looking me in the eye: "Of course, these are still your ideas, Tom."

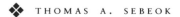 THOMAS A. SEBEOK

Optimism

Several years ago, Dr. Wells was discussing the best location for a swimming pool he wanted to build for his relaxation and therapeutic program. Two locations were under consideration—Meadowood and his home on East Tenth Street. Sensing that some people might doubt the long-term need for a Wells swimming pool, he paused. "I guess it's okay for me to build a pool. After all, Mother was looking for growth stocks when she was 94! This is my version of her optimism!"

Rhubarb Pie

RECENTLY, I asked Dr. Wells to make a call to a key advisor to a major benefactor about a project we were presenting for a seven-figure gift. On my way home from Indianapolis, I stopped at Gray's Cafeteria in Mooresville to survey the selection of pies and bought a rhubarb pie for Dr. Wells. When I visited at his home, I found Dr. Wells taking his daily swim and, crouching on the deck of the pool, I told him how important his call had been and gave his houseboy the rhubarb pie. Dr. Wells called out to me as I left, "If the reward is rhubarb pie, I'll make as many calls as you like!"

CURT SIMIC

The Stahr Report

MY first glimpse of Herman B Wells was in either 1940 or 1941. He was the Commencement speaker at the University of Kentucky, and I was in the audience, seated too high in the stadium to see him clearly, but I well remember a solid-looking figure with a black mustache and a friendly voice.

I met him in the fifties a couple of times at higher-education conferences, and we became pretty well acquainted. In the fall of 1961, when I was under consideration as his possible successor at Indiana University, we had lunch together in Washington. We talked about the University, of course. He was in his twenty-fifth year as President of his Alma Mater, and he obviously loved her deeply. But having been both a leading participant in and a keen observer of American academia, he knew a number of cases in which a retiring president had been so reluctant to "let go" that he made things needlessly tough for his successor and, thus, for the institution itself. So he made it a point to say this: "Elvis, I want you to know that if you become President of Indiana University, I shall not set foot in the Administration Building even once for at least your first year, nor will I call you on the phone. I'll give you my full support; I'll always be on the other end of the line if you want to call me, but I'll never interfere."

He was true to his word. With one exception, I saw him only on social or ceremonial occasions or at football games for at least a year, but long before I left we became fast friends—we still are; and my wife and our children also came to love him— and we all still do. As far as I know, he never criticized anything I did, controversial though some of my actions were. His mother, that wonderful Mrs. Granville Wells, became almost like a mother to my wife, too, and helped make her feel thoroughly welcome and at home in this new setting.

The exception I referred to was at meetings of the Indiana University Foundation. It was traditional for the University President to be Chairman of the Board of the Foundation. The Board elected me Chairman in 1962, but it had the good sense to elect Herman President of the Foundation, and neither of us missed a Board meeting during my entire time there.

At least one of those meetings each year was held somewhere other than Bloomington, usually an attractive place such as Scottsdale where a Board member could play host. Always, however, it had to be held where there was a swimming pool handy, for even then Herman loved a daily dip.

Indiana University was nationally regarded as a leading bastion of academic freedom when I arrived there, not least because of Herman Wells' strong and successful earlier defense of the Kinsey Institute against enormous outside pressures. That tradition of a free marketplace of ideas, which owed so much to his twenty-five unwavering years, was of incalculable importance to the University in the mid- to late sixties, when academic freedom was coming under severe and sustained attack from extremists on the left all across the land, as it had from the far right in the McCarthy era in the fifties.

Herman has a subtle sense of humor, and it sometimes would

sort of sneak up on me. In talking about Alfred Kinsey, who had founded the Institute for Research in Human Sexuality, but who had died before I could know him, he once said, "Elvis, Professor Kinsey was a genuine scholar. He lectured on the most fascinating subject in the world, but he could make it sound dry as dust."

 ELVIS J. STAHR, JR.

Safe Driver?

AFTER many years of experience driving automobiles, I had come to prize myself as a very good fast driver. When I first started working for Acting President Wells, there were times when I did not think that I was fast enough to make the speed that he himself could make behind the steering wheel over the winding highway between Indianapolis and Bloomington. Consequently, while en route traveling a little late, occasionally he would tell me to let him have the wheel and for me to hang on so that he could make up for the tardiness. Frequently, I felt that even with both of my hands latched to the side of the Ford touring car I was not quite sure. It was hard to be comfortably oriented either physically or mentally for the rapid zig-zagging, but I survived the conditioning, and I concluded that Acting President Wells was the fastest and safest driver on a continuously curving highway that I had known.

JOHN STEWART

A Gallon of Sorghum

IN 1969, the not-for-profit organizations and foundations were seriously threatened by proposed legislation in Washington caused by unwise actions by certain foundations. A group of private and public foundations undertook the task of lobbying to channel the legislation into a more constructive approach with suggested solutions to the problem. However, very little progress had occurred. A group including Father Hesburgh of Notre Dame, Chancellor Wells, and other university and foundation presidents went to Washington to testify before the Senate Finance Committee.

Herman had a carefully prepared package and he asked me to carry it for him, which I gladly did. When we arrived at the committee hearing a few minutes before it started, Herman walked down the aisle. I accompanied him to the platform with the now opened package. After exchanging greetings with the Chairman, Senator Russell Long, Louisiana, Chancellor Wells said, "Russell, I have brought you a gallon of good Brown County sorghum." Long reached for the gallon container, replying, "That will be great on my grits each morning, Herman," and adding, "What brings you here?" Long put the sorghum bucket on the table by his gavel.

Wells explained he had come to testify on behalf of the foundations, museums, hospitals, universities, and so on, against the then current proposals in the bill that would make it difficult for charitable and not-for-profit organizations to exist.

Chairman Long said, "Good, we'll put you on first."

The Wells testimony was most effective. I had witnessed again, as I have on numerous occasions, the marvelous persuasive powers of Herman as to the significant role he has played in preserving and enhancing the unique role of the charitable (not-for-profit) organizations in our society.

 RICHARD B. STONER

A Threatened Witch-Hunt

How does one account for the fact that, all during the infamous McCarthy era, Indiana University was singularly spared what so many other universities came to be so unhappily subjected to? After all, no McCarthy and no Jenner committees ever descended upon the I.U. campus; no faculty members were subjected to public interrogations; and none came to be branded as either Communists or "5th Amendment pleaders." And why not? Well, it was largely due to President Herman B Wells' exceedingly adroit way of deflecting at least one such threatened witch-hunt early in the game.

At issue was an attack on two members of the I.U. faculty at Bloomington. It was several months before the fall elections; the Communist Party in Indiana (the Party was still not illegal at that time) had managed to secure enough signatures to a petition that the names of their Communist Party candidates be included on the ballot in the next elections. Following all the required legal procedures, the petition was delivered to the Secretary of State, who was then required by law to have the names printed on the ballot. But the Secretary of State simply laughed the whole thing off, saying that he was never going to have the names of any Communists printed on any ballot, even though it was required by law that he do so; and if the Communist Party wished to bring suit in the courts, they could go right ahead; but by the time the case could ever come to be adjudicated, the fall elections would have been held and be over with, and "What good would that then do the 'Commies,' " he is reported to have said.

This cynical disregard of the law aroused two eminent members of the I.U. Law faculty: Bernard Gavit, Dean of the Law School, and Fowler Harper. Both Gavit and Harper undertook to mount a vigorous campaign, largely through the newspapers, to try to bring the pressure of public opinion to bear on the Secretary of State to carry out his stated duties under the law.

And what was the reaction? The American Legion, headquartered in Indianapolis, became very exercised on the score of one of their favorite issues—namely, that of anti-Communism. The officers of the Legion called upon the Governor, and demanded that he launch an investigation of Communist influences among the I.U. faculty in Bloomington. The Governor caved in to Legion pressure, and officially requested Herman B Wells to institute the investigation of the I.U. faculty.

No sooner was the news of this official request by the Governor prominently played up in the newspapers, than the faculty at I.U. were very much up in arms! It was insulting to the very integrity and loyalty of the faculty, we said, that the Governor should have thus given in to the demands of the Legion, and should have ordered so unwarranted and so outrageous an investigation. We even made informal representations to President Wells that he should refuse to honor so outrageous a request from the Governor.

Imagine, then, our consternation and dismay when, instead of firing the request right back in the Governor's face, President Wells was all smiles! "Of course, Indiana University would welcome such an investigation," he said in effect, "and would do all that it could to facilitate the investigation in every way!" At this, we naive faculty champions, who had so eagerly rallied round the banner of "No witch-hunts at I.U.!" felt not just let down, but even betrayed. The only trouble was, we quite failed to heed the whole of what President Wells had said in his response! For after insisting that I.U. welcomed the investigation, President Wells had then said in effect, "But first of all, since it is the Legion who has made the accusation, we would appreciate it if the Legion would come forward and present us with any actual evidence that they have of there having been either any Communist infiltration or any Communist sympathizers on the faculty."

This quite caught the Legion off guard! They had no evidence at all! Finally, the Legion stumblingly and fumblingly blurted out to the newspapers something to the effect that some three or four years before, one of the programs of the I.U. Auditorium Series had been a concert by Paul Robeson! And was it not generally known that Robeson was at least a Communist sympathizer?

Well, that did it! For even Hoosier newspaper readers came to feel that, in its effort to embarrass the I.U. faculty and administration with charges of Communism, it was the Legion, not the University, that had come out with egg on its face. Nor seemingly was the lesson lost on potential future witch-hunters, once the Mc-Carthy era came into full swing. For as I noted earlier, I.U. was notably spared when it came to such disrupting and embarrassing investigations as so many other colleges and universities later had to suffer from. But not so I.U. For doubtless any future Red-baiters learned their lesson from the Legion's early embarrass-ment, when they had tried to take on I.U., and found themselves completely outmaneuvered by so adroit a tactician as Herman Wells.

Nor was it only the witch-hunters who learned their lesson when it came to making precipitate criticisms of I.U. and the Wells administration. No, for we eager younger faculty members also, who had been so ready to wave the flag of academic free-dom and to force things to an issue—we too learned our lesson. For again, it was Herman Wells who taught us that often it is far better to give ground at first, in order thereby to gain ground eventually and in the long run.

 HENRY B. VEATCH

Salmon Soufflé

CHANCELLOR Herman Wells was intrigued in Frankfort when he heard that the George E. Powells and the Waters hoped to get a reservation to dine at L'Auberge de L'Ill in Illhaeusern on a cou-ple days' notice instead of months. François Delachaux, a good friend of I.U. and Chef Hasberlin, called for us. The famed restau-rant was sold out but a small private dining room would be opened.

The food was as phenomenal as ever. Indeed, I often wondered if God sent down to the earth on Friday nights to have an order of salmon soufflé sent up. All ate with great zest and no one any more so than Herman B. Indeed, there were a few bits of salmon and considerable sauce on the tray. The service had been a little below the usual standards and the head waitress was somewhat dour. Chancellor Wells thought we should finish the platter, although there was scarcely enough for a second serving for a single person. Because his right arm was still in a sling, he couldn't very well service anyone else or himself but he picked up the platter. About that time, the waitress did step forth to help and he gave her a smile of appreciation like I have never seen in my life. Suddenly, her grim look was transformed into a thing of beauty. All others turned down an additional spoonful, although there was considerable self-sacrifice on my part. The scene ended with the waitress holding the platter at an angle while Chancellor Wells picked up a piece of superb French bread and swabbed all of the sauce and scraps onto his plate.

Names, Again

IN 1956 I had the pleasure of introducing Chancellor Wells to nine young, distinguished visitors from six countries of Europe. They visited for a half hour or so. One month later we were gathered in the old Campus Club and one of my friends, Chris Diakopoulos, spotted Chancellor Wells across the room. He said, "Oh, there is the Chancellor." I said, "Yes, he'll probably come over and visit with us." Chris replied, "Do you think he will know us?" I answered, "Of course, and I'll bet you a dollar he will call you by name." Chris replied, "This is ridiculous. I have met him only once and he hasn't seen me for a month. The bet is on." About that time, the Chancellor came over, put out his hand, and said, "Good day, Mr. Diakopoulos. How are you getting along?"

Room at the Inn

WE were on the same plane going to Washington, D.C., and took a cab to the Mayflower Hotel. The time was about 6:30 p.m. I had a guaranteed reservation and rarely stayed at the Mayflower. Chancellor Wells was delayed a bit by acquaintances in the lobby. I was assigned my room and noted that he was having a bit of difficulty over his. He protested some, saying that there was a letter on file; that his reservations were always guaranteed. The assistant manager, who had been called by the desk clerk, apologized and said he was sorry but they would get him a room in a nearby hotel. I volunteered my room but he declined. About that time, a couple of bellhops, who overheard the discussion, stepped forward and spoke out. Apparently, the assistant manager was new and he was swarmed over by about three bellhops who said, "You can't do this to Dr. Wells; he always stays here." The insubordination was so shocking and sincere that the manager relented but said, "I sure don't know what I'm going to do for someone else who has been assigned that room."

The Wells Diet

I always enjoyed Chancellor Wells' remark that dieting was easy— he had lost 600 pounds. On one occasion, he was at a reception in our home. He was on a bit of a diet and was standing with his back to a table where a variety of incredibly rich hors d'oeuvres was available. His right hand went behind his back and unerringly moved directly to the tidbits with a delicacy matched only by the prehensile talent of the tip of an elephant's trunk. I never saw such accuracy and I think that on this occasion he didn't follow his eating regimen.

Academic Freedom

I was testifying in a rate case before the Public Service Commission of Indiana on behalf of the public. The chief attorney for the utility was Roger Branigan, a trustee of Purdue and later Governor of Indiana. Branigan thought it singularly improper for me to be testifying and when he saw Chancellor Wells, he said, "A member of your faculty is testifying against a corporation which is one of my clients; in fact, I am going to cross-examine him tomorrow." Wells remarked, according to Branigan, that I should find the experience stimulating. Branigan responded, "If he were at Purdue, he couldn't do it." Wells replied, "What a pity!"

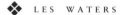

LES   WATERS

Man of Culture

Dr. Herman Wells is known as a man of great culture, who not only supports artistic endeavor because of its contribution to the quality of life of humankind, but also because he personally is stimulated and moved by artistic creation. We in the School of Music are constantly inspired by his presence at many musical events. One of my favorite remembrances occurred on the occasion of a performance of Verdi's *Requiem* in the Musical Arts Center several years ago.

I happened to see Dr. Wells as we were entering the auditorium together, and he said to me, "Charles, I have an important meeting to attend later in the evening, so when you see me leave the performance, it is not because I am not enjoying it but simply because I have to be somewhere else." I replied that I understood completely and was grateful for his attendance even for a brief period of time.

After the concert was over, whom did I see but Dr. Wells! I commented to him that I was surprised to see him there because he had indicated earlier that he had to go to a meeting. "I should be at a meeting at this time," he said, "but the performance was so beautiful and compelling I simply could not tear myself away."

❖ CHARLES WEBB

Indiana, Our Indiana

BY 1981, when I was asked by the Union Board to introduce him at its annual pre-Purdue football game dinner, Herman Wells was a universally respected and beloved figure at the University and throughout higher education. He had traveled a long distance since 1937 when *Time Magazine* reported "Nashville playboy chosen I.U. prexy!" I remember that quote well—and used it in my introduction that night—because the description was so unlike the man he had become.

Chancellor Wells had recently chronicled his years as president of Indiana University in a book entitled *Being Lucky*. The speech he had been asked to give that night was a repeat of a highly successful address he had delivered during the summer at the School of Continuing Studies/Alumni Association's Mini University which might have been entitled *Being Lucky: What Was Left Out*. Included in that presentation were details of his meetings with such people as the Shah of Iran, Haile Selassie, and J. Paul Getty.

Upon concluding his prepared remarks he changed directions and related another story with equal, if not more, pleasure. He explained that he had had the opportunity that summer to hang a medallion around the neck of the oldest living I.U. graduate, who had been, incidentally, over 100 years old and very short. He described how, when he placed the medallion around her neck, she had looked up at him and had begun to sing "Indiana, Our Indiana." The room became very quiet as he informed the audience with great feeling that the woman had since passed away and gone to the great beyond—with "Indiana, Our Indiana" on her lips. Eyes filled with tears as he finished the tale by emotionally confiding that he prayed when he went to his reward that he would have the song on his lips and he had the same wish for everyone in the crowd.

Silence and more tears greeted the end of his talk. Then the crowd broke into fervent applause. As Chancellor Wells sat down he leaned over to me and whispered, "Jim, you don't think that ending was too shmaltzy do you?" Coming from anyone else, the answer would probably be yes. But not from him. Not from the man who spoke with equal passion about the Shah of Iran and I.U.'s oldest living alum. And not from the man who had so clearly outgrown that 1937 epithet, "Nashville playboy!"

Santa Claus

THOUGH busy as always, Chancellor Wells made time to attend the annual School of Continuing Studies Christmas reception one year in the late 1980s. However, prior commitments forced him to appear wearing his beloved Santa Claus suit. This caused no particular stir as everyone was accustomed to seeing Chancellor Wells in this attire since he has played Santa Claus for many years for groups throughout the campus. The only hitch came when the Chancellor tried to sample the food on the buffet. His beard was in the way. This problem was solved when he pulled the beard down, which made him look a little strange but allowed him to eat.

When the time came for him to leave, we were concerned about the cold weather and asked the Chancellor if his driver, John, had arrived. With a twinkle in his eye he said, "No, but my sleigh and reindeer await me!"

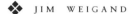 JIM WEIGAND

Taking Chances

IN 1949, I received a telephone call from President Herman B Wells inviting me to become Executive Director of the Indiana University Foundation. I had graduated in 1942, spent nearly five years in the U.S. Army, and almost three years in the advertising business. What he saw in me that even suggested that I might be able to help the Foundation, I will never know. Furthermore, how he convinced the Foundation's distinguished Board of Directors that they should rely upon the judgment of a 29-year-old graduate remains a mystery to me.

Be that as it may, I will forever be grateful to him for having that confidence and, furthermore, for lending his "weight" to some of the steps I proposed and implemented.

When I recommended an "Annual Giving" program and put together a brochure asking all alumni to contribute $1.00 to the Foundation, one of the directors pointed out that they had hired me to raise thousands of dollars, not $1.00. Dr. Wells supported my proposal and that mailing brought in $27,000.

When I recommended that we get the students involved and proposed a Student Foundation Committee, he hosted a lovely dinner for some thirty-five outstanding juniors and seniors. They took the challenge and the rest is history.

When I suggested a bicycle race—to keep the student committee interested and challenged—he recommended it to the directors. As I remember, the idea received less than an enthusiastic endorsement from the board. He even paid $5.00 for his own ticket to the first race. He also hosted an after-race party at his home to thank all the volunteers who helped make the first race a rewarding success.

Although I only worked for Herman Wells three years, those three years were as satisfying and as rewarding as anyone could hope for. Herman took a chance, I took a chance, and I like to think that we both won.

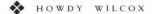 HOWDY WILCOX

Ripples

STORIES abound about Herman Wells' "personal touch." Like everything else during his presidency, this important part was not the result of "being lucky" but rather of "being thoughtful." For instance, when President Wells wanted to meet with a colleague, often he would go to his or her office. When possible, the meeting would be scheduled just after the change of classes, and the President would have an opportunity to greet students along the way. "Hi, how are you?" "What's your name?" "Where are you from?" "Oh, do you know the Bob Smiths from there? Wonderful folks!"

The students loved it! They told their sweethearts; they told their friends; they told their families—all of whom told others. The ripple effect enhanced reality, and soon President Wells was believed to be everywhere and to know everyone's name and home town.

Isn't there a somewhat similar story about bread and fish in the Bible?

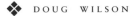 DOUG WILSON

The Gates on Kirkwood Avenue

I remember vividly one conversation with Dr. Wells as a lesson in friendship, politics, and the value of patience. Not ordinary mortal patience, but the real, life-long patience that builds lasting institutions.

Halfway through my term as Student Trustee in 1978 I met with Dr. Wells to check on how I was doing. We met on a Sunday in his office in Owen Hall, after he had been to church. It was a bright winter morning, and I will always remember the sunbeams shining through the front windows and gleaming off Dr. Wells' white hair.

After talking about a number of subjects the nagging problem of the "Kirkwood gates" came up. It seemed that for several years wealthy alumni had proposed building gates at the entrance to the campus on Kirkwood Avenue. Each time the idea became public, students protested that there were better ways than to spend money on "some old posts in the ground."

Jeff Richardson, one of my friends and a student on the City Council, had been particularly vocal about the gates. When Jeff was student body president he organized protests against the gates. The alumni grew so upset that they withdrew their money altogether, and wouldn't give anything to the University. I tended to side with Jeff, and wondered if the Trustees could get the alums to give their money for scholarships.

"Don't worry about those gates," Dr. Wells replied. "And don't worry about Jeff, either. Jeff is a good friend of mine, too, but on this one I think you two may be wrong." Dr. Wells' eyes twinkled in the morning sun, and when he laughed he sounded every bit the part of Santa Claus he played for the Union.

"You see," he chuckled, "I have left the money for those gates in my own will, and unless somebody else steps forward, I will get those gates on Kirkwood built. I'll get the last laugh, and you and Jeff will enjoy those gates for years to come. Alumni give money for what they want—not always what we want—and we just have to be patient."

Of course, later my fraternity brother Ed Sample did donate money for the Kirkwood gates. Jeff Richardson and I have stayed close friends in politics—in different parties—over the years. And thanks to Brother Sample, we have all enjoyed the splendid Sample Gates on Kirkwood.

Tainted Money

WHEN discussing whether we should accept gifts to the Campaign for Indiana from tobacco companies, Dr. Wells repeated his advice on money for universities: "The only 'tainted' money is 'taint enough!'"

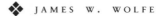 JAMES W. WOLFE

Family Affair

IT must have been in the 1960s, I was informed that the faculty had rejected a proposal Herman had made that all those who were tenured, and had not earned any of his or her degrees in courses at Indiana University, be awarded an honorary I.U. master's degree, traditionally the historic teaching degree. Thus all who had suffered "deprivation" would be bonded and banded even closer in the University family than tenure alone signified. If I have mis-remembered or even invented some of this, no doubt Chancellor Wells, with his capacious and prodigious memory, would be able to set the record straight!

I suggest that every officer who ever had even a modicum of success in serving Indiana University has walked, knowingly or not, haltingly or boldly, in the path blazed by Herman B Wells.

   LESTER M. WOLFSON

Contributors

WILLIAM S. ARMSTRONG, former President, Indiana University Foundation

RONALD G. BALLENGER, houseboy for Herman B Wells, 1964–1968; Chief, Family Support Division, U.S. Army, Munich, Germany

JOHN V. BARNETT, former President, Indiana University Alumni Association

GERALD L. BEPKO, Vice President, Indiana University; Chancellor, Indiana University–Purdue University at Indianapolis

CHARLES F. BONSER, Director, Regional Economic Development Institute; Professor of Public and Environmental Affairs, and of Business Administration

OTIS R. BOWEN, former Governor, State of Indiana

SAMUEL E. BRADEN, Professor Emeritus of Economics

ROBERT E. BURTON, former Secretary, Indiana University Board of Trustees

ROBERT F. BYRNES, Distinguished Professor Emeritus of History

JAMES H. CAPSHEW, houseboy for Herman B Wells, 1977–1979; Assistant Professor, Department of History and Philosophy of Science, Indiana University

DONALD F. CARMONY, Professor Emeritus of History

THOMAS D. CLARK, Distinguished Professor Emeritus of History

DOTTIE COLLINS, Editorial Assistant to the Chancellor

WAYNE O. CRAIG, Director of University Ceremonies

D. C. "DANNY" DANIELSON, former Trustee, Indiana University

HARRY G. DAY, Professor Emeritus of Chemistry

MARY PAUL DIETERLE, widow of Lyle Dieterle, Professor Emeritus of Accounting

THOMAS EHRLICH, President, Indiana University

BYRON K. ELLIOTT, Emeritus Member, Indiana University Foundation Board of Directors

JAMES M. ELLIOTT, former Vice President, Indiana University Foundation

ROBERT H. FERRELL, Distinguished Professor Emeritus of History

J. A. FRANKLIN, JR., Director, Federal Relations, Indiana University

JOHN GALLMAN, Director, Indiana University Press

GEORGE N. GILL, Emeritus Member, Indiana University Foundation Board of Directors

MARY REES GILLIATT, wife of Neal Gilliatt, Indiana University Foundation Board of Directors

HARRY L. GONSO, Trustee, Indiana University

ROSANN R. GREENE, former University Director of Faculty Records

KENNETH R. R. GROS LOUIS, Vice President, Indiana University; Chancellor, Indiana University Bloomington

CAROL S. GROSS, Secretary, Indiana University Foundation Board of Directors

CHARLES HARRELL, former Secretary, Indiana University Board of Trustees

MAYNARD K. HINE, former Dean, Indiana University School of Dentistry

HARRIETT AND RICHARD INSKEEP, Mrs. Inskeep former Trustee, Indiana University

GLENN W. IRWIN, JR., Chancellor Emeritus, Indiana University–Purdue University at Indianapolis; Dean Emeritus and Professor Emeritus, Indiana University School of Medicine

PAUL G. JASPER, former President, Indiana University Alumni Association

FRANK B. JONES, former Director, Indiana University Alumni Association

JOANNE B. LANTZ, Chancellor, Indiana University–Purdue University at Fort Wayne

ELEANOR R. LONG, wife of Professor Newell H. Long, Professor Emeritus of Music

NEWELL H. LONG, Professor Emeritus of Music

ROBERT A. LUCAS, former Trustee, Indiana University

DOROTHY McCREA, widow of Robert McCrea, former Trustee, Indiana University

PAUL P. MASSA, JR., houseboy for Herman B Wells, 1960-1962; President, Congressional Information Service, Inc., Bethesda, Maryland

HANSI MENDEL, long-time friend of Herman B Wells

ROBERT H. MENKE, former Trustee, Indiana University

THOMAS M. MILLER, member, Indiana University Foundation Board of Directors

TROY MURRAY-PLUMER, houseboy for Herman B Wells, 1989-1990; attends the Cooley School of Law in Michigan

ROBERT C. PEBWORTH, former President, Indiana University Alumni Association

RUDY POZZATTI, Distinguished Professor Emeritus of Fine Arts

CLAUDE RICH, former Director, Indiana University Alumni Association

DOW RICHARDSON, former President, Indiana University Alumni Association

JOHN W. RYAN, President Emeritus of Indiana University; Professor of Political Science, and of Public and Environmental Affairs

THOMAS A. SEBEOK, Distinguished Professor Emeritus of Linguistics and Semiotics; Professor Emeritus of Anthropology, and of Uralic and Altaic Studies

CURT SIMIC, President, Indiana University Foundation

ELVIS J. STAHR, JR., former President, Indiana University

JOHN L. STEWART, houseboy for Herman B Wells, 1937-1940, the first to serve in that capacity; was a longtime teacher and administrator at North Carolina College, Durham.

RICHARD B. STONER, President, Indiana University Board of Trustees

HENRY B. VEATCH, former Distinguished Service Professor of Philosophy

LESLIE WATERS, University Professor Emeritus of Transportation and Business History

CHARLES WEBB, Dean, Indiana University School of Music

JAMES WEIGAND, Dean, Indiana University School of Continuing Studies; Professor of Education

HOWARD S. "HOWDY" WILCOX, former Trustee, Indiana University

DOUGLAS M. WILSON, Vice President for University Relations and External Affairs, Indiana University

JAMES W. WOLFE, former Trustee, Indiana University

LESTER M. WOLFSON, Chancellor Emeritus, Indiana University at South Bend